Philosophic Play on Culture and Society

Other Works by Sandy Krolick

Вероника: Сибирская Сказка (Novel)
VERONIKA: The Siberian's Tale (Novel)
The Recovery of Ecstasy: Notebooks from Siberia
Apocalypse of the Barbarians: Inquisitions on Empire
Conversations On A Country Path
Gandhi in the Postmodern Age
Recollective Resolve
Ethical Decision-making Styles
Культурныи критицизм
Myth, Mystery and Magic: Religious Imagination in Ancient Egypt
Russian Soul and Collapse of the West
Shambhala (Novel)
Misha (Novel)
On Being and Being Good
Q: Interpreting QAnon
A New Heaven and a New Earth

Philosophic Play on Culture and Society

sandy krolick, ph.d

Islands Press
New York : Altai Krai

ISBN: 978-1-7350698-5-2

Cover art courtesy of:
Yuri Ivanov
Altai Krai, Russia

Maturity is regaining the seriousness of child's play

Friederich Nietzsche

In the Folds of the Flesh
Reflections On Touch

> Because such fingers need to knit
> That subtle knot which makes us man,
> So must pure lovers' souls descend
> T' affections, and to faculties,
> Which sense may reach and apprehend,
> Else a great prince in prison lies.
> To our bodies turn we then, that so
> Weak men on love reveal'd may look;
> Love's mysteries in souls do grow,
> But yet the body is his book.

John Donne, *The Ecstasy*

A Tactile Ontology

Following a path charted by the late Hans Jonas, any inquiry concerning our sense of touch must proceed on two concurrent paths; first from the vantage point of agency, and secondly from the perspective of the percipient body. In other words, we need to grasp our haptic sensibility in terms of its spontaneous movement between acting on the one hand and feeling on the other. We must try to articulate how in its very intentionality — extending oneself, bodying-forth, reaching-out, or embracing someone — touch is both 'open-to' and 'receptive-of,' eliciting response from within the very folds of the flesh. Jonas makes the following comment concerning this ontological priority of the feeling body's engagement in the world.

The living body that can die, that has a world and itself belongs to the world, that feels and itself can be felt... this body is a memento of the still unsolved question of ontology 'What is being'? (1)

Now, if Jonas is correct, and I believe he is, then understanding the phenomenon of touch will require an ontology of the flesh, of the body itself — as both subject and object of tactile experience. In short, human existence must be understood in terms of embodiment first and foremost — one's capacity to touch and to be touched, to feel and to be felt, to hear and to be heard. Maurice Merleau-Ponty agrees when he writes: "I delve into the thickness of the world by perceptual experience."(2) We now seek to articulate the very earthiness of this all-to-human ontology from within the 'thickness' of the flesh itself.

And The Word Became Flesh

The primacy of touch in human relations was somewhat recently thrown into high relief as a result of the novel coronavirus circulating among us, along with the on-again, off-again periods of isolation and the attendant loneliness suffered in its wake. In point of fact, a person cannot long ignore the pleadings of the flesh or the deep-seated need for touch in everyday relations. Similarly, one cannot fail to recognize the continuous and deliberate attenuation of both in the increasingly virtualized life-world that had come to characterize life in society today. So we ask at first: Is not touch my body's original experience of itself as it palpates the world? While my eyes may engage things and other persons through mediated palpation, touch presupposes the immediacy of contact — of friction, of resistance — the pressure of my body against another physical presence within my environment.

What I had previously read while browsing Vladimir Dal's nineteenth century work, *An Explanatory Dictionary of the Russian Language*, simply confirmed what I already had learned from a decade living on the Siberian taiga — that is to say, I came to grasp more fully the primacy of touch. According to Dal's lexicography, our five senses could easily be reduced to haptic perception alone: the tongue and palate, touching food; the ear, touching sound waves; the nose, touching emanations; and the eyes, touching rays of light. The sense of touch would thus appear to define the very interstices of my world through location, movement, and the reach of my flesh — both inline and outline of the lived-body-world simultaneously. As my late professor Paul Ricoeur might have stated when quoting his countryman Maurice Merleau-Ponty, flesh is a chiasm, the intersecting of body-as-subject and world-as-lived by the body, affording me the very possibility of tactile experience — of touching and being touched. Quoting D. Katz in *Der Aufbau der Tastwelt*, he writes:

[T]he movement of one's own body is to touch what lighting is to vision… And like the exploratory gaze of true vision, the 'knowing touch' projects us outside our body through movement. When one of my hands touches the other, the end that moves functions as subject and the other as object. (3)

In other words, in the phenomenon of touch we discover a natural intertwining of self and world, of self and Other. And as Merleau-Ponty further points out: "I cannot forget in this case that it is through my body that I go to the world."(4) In fact, as he concludes,

Experience discloses beneath objective space, in which the body eventually finds its place, a primitive spatiality of which experience is merely the outer covering and which merges with the body's very being. To be a body is to be tied to a certain world. (5)

My body then articulates itself spatially vis-a-vis my comportment within the world; my eyes opening into a world which touches, receives and includes them; my gaze encountering things already there, standing out within an encompassing horizon. Looking out into this horizon, something appears, a certain determinacy occurs. As my sight continues to focus, objects take on specific shape and size; they reveal a natural spatiality. But the presence of such objects within my visual field only occur because I am not simply a gaze; I too am spatially present. "Not primarily in space, but of it," I am always, already attuned within a world through my body-as-subject.(6) As embodied, the movements and postures I assume both constitute and are constituted by the world that touches me as I reach out and touch it. There is a natural reciprocity or openness to the flesh: touching, I am also touched — both actor and recipient, subject and object of the sensation at one and the same time. Here is the true entwining of self and other, at the interstice of my body of flesh and the flesh of the world.

Even prior to opening her eyes, a newborn feels her body through the intimacy of a mother's embrace — that is, through the sense of touch. Beginning with that first caress, the world becomes a sensual playground for her infinitely excitable flesh. For this infant, even the inanimate objects of her surroundings, what we adults might call dead matter — a stone, a tree, wind, water, fire and ice — even these phenomena are alive under her gaze, and under her touch; they are filled with life, passion, and being — just as they were for our primeval forbearers, where vitality was everywhere, and being was the same as being alive. As Jonas reminds us;

> *Though this is forgotten, the cosmos was once alive as perceived by man, and its more recent lifeless image was built up, or left over, in a continuous process of critical subtraction from fuller original content. (7)*

What we moderns dismissively label animism or vitalism — the attributing of life and intention to inanimate objects or nature — was for the many millennia of pre-civilized hominid existence a simple acknowledgement of the power, the force, the capacity of nature to act; and since we are intimately part of that nature, it is a recognition of the power enabling our own movement as well. Insofar as all things share in this ability, this pouvoir, we are basically of the same essence, the same substance. I became acutely aware of this while being resident in Siberia, living closer to the land — to nature and its power — understanding that we are part of the earth, the soil, as it is part of us; we share the same flesh, the same destiny.

Even my own body does not initially present me as an isolated entity, separate from the world — like some Cartesian ego locked up within a bag of skin. Rather, my flesh articulates my facticity as well as my tactility — a dwelling place within the powerful continuum of life. Neither am I simply a static presence within this field. I too exhibit motility and intentionality; a spontaneous capacity to move and to engage — the act of touch itself suggestive of such inherent potency along with the dynamic configuration of space, as realized in dance, in the hunt, and in play, as well as in eating, sleeping, and sexual engagement.

From the simple positioning of my body, whether passively suffering or forcibly acting, my flesh exhibits a natural reflexivity, a turning back upon itself, both the breach and bridge that constitute my being-situated. This somatic facing in two directions, both inward (proprioceptive), and outward (tactile), is the ground of my own ecstatic existence; it is a pre-reflective experience of doubling, whereby I understand the potentiality of being both myself and being other than myself, immersed in the power of life: my flesh, the flesh of the world! As Richard Kearney reminds us in his little book, entitled Touch.

Body and mind are like the inside and outside of our skin—two sides of one sleeve. And since tactuality is what allows for empathy with others, a civilization that loses touch with flesh loses touch with itself. (8)

Tactility and Empathy

In this, our current post-modern predicament, the question must now be raised: have we already lost touch with our senses, with ourselves? Have we lost touch with the flesh as well as with one another? Recall what Adam and Eve had discovered back in Big

Daddy's garden of earthly delights — nakedness, intimacy, sexuality — the feeling of flesh against flesh; a primal act perhaps more eloquently expressed by the poet.

When love with one another so inter-
aminates two souls ...
So must pure lovers' souls descend
to affections, and to faculties
Which sense may reach and apprehend. (9)

This question then — of losing touch with ourselves and our capacity for touch — lies at the very foundation of our current dilemma, a situation made yet more poignant and impactful through the inconveniences created by a novel coronavirus. But perhaps, just perhaps, there's a remnant, a small crease in our historic march to a post-Covid world, that still allows for our being-with-one-another, intimately engaged, touching and being touched.

However, we should first understand that touch is not always or only about physical contact or communion per-se, but also being 'in-touch' as well; this is a much broader medium of engagement or 'being-with' the Other. As Kearney intimated above: there's a sense in which touch is also feeling-for, caring-for, or empathically being-with the Other. This may be why our most primal forbearers sensed their own totemic identifications not simply as metaphors, but rather as a means of genuine engagement-with and being touched by something larger than themselves, the experience of having an identity greater than oneself, attached to something more — a Platonic metaxis — an "in-betweenness" or in Victor Turner's terminology, a liminal state. And, perhaps touch or tactile intimacy within the most primal of human communities was not simply a matter of flesh upon flesh; although it was surely that as well. (10) Rather, it may be as much about the natural folding-in or conjoining of oneself symbolically with the Other as seen in relations adhering among most kinship-based societies.

In kin relationships, others become predicates of one's own existence, and vice versa… It is the integration of certain relationships, hence the participation of certain others in one's own being. As members of one another, kinsmen live each other's lives and die each other's deaths... [I]n kinship, as in relations to the cosmos in general, alterity is a condition of the possibility of being. (11)

In such settings, the very notion of self as an isolated ego — a relatively unspoken assumption undergirding our modern conception of individuality — was either non-existent or not of primary concern among our pre-modern predecessors. In fact, in kinship-grounded cultures the individual was meaningfully constituted only in his or her tangible (felt) relations with other members of the tribe or clan, including a rather fluid identity shared among totem and tribe within their natural surround. Here we may note, for example, that encounters with ancestral spirits among the Amazonian Piraha — whether in dream or awake — were as real as any concrete relations between tribal members themselves. (12)   In fact, within most pre-civilized cultures, the person is rarely if ever seen as a purely independent, isolated interiority struggling against a foreign environment. Rather, the individual exists as an embodied instantiation of a much more encompassing sense of self-in-community. As Marshall Sahlins reminds us:

Ethnographic reports speak of 'transpersonal self' (Native Americans), of self as a 'locus of shared social relations or shared biographies'(Caroline Islands), of persons as 'the plural and composite site of the relationships that produced them' (New Guinea Highlands). Referring broadly to the African concept of 'the individual,' Roger Bastide writes: 'He does not exist except to the extent he is outside and different from himself.' Clearly, the self in these societies is not synonymous with the bounded, unitary and autonomous individual as we know him... Rather the individual person is the locus of multiple other selves with whom he or she is joined in mutual relations of being... (13)

Of course there are other examples among pre-urban and pre-literate cultures, far too numerous to recount, where departed kinsmen, helper spirits, or other phantom guides, engage auditorily, visually, and even tactilely with those still among the living — with countrymen, friends, family, shamans, priests, or visionaries. In short, embodiment in one form or another — being touched, in-touch, or even touching the hand of God — remains central to our human tragedy. And, remember that even the risen Jesus of Nazareth appeared to his disciples in the flesh.

The Frailty of Flesh

There's an important distinction still to be drawn between simple tactile sensations and the unparalleled feeling of flesh upon flesh. The impressions I receive when I reach out and touch something are not quite the same as what I experience when I feel or embrace another person. And this is the real mystery of the flesh, where a "mere touch-impression" is transformed from a simple "tactile encounter" to "feeling another body." (14)

Touching another person elicits a singular sensation, originating in the natural reflexivity of the act itself. Touching the Other, I am acutely aware of how he or she feels when being touched by me. This experiencing of one's own flesh in and through touching or being touched by another is at the heart of our experience of sexual intimacy. In no other tactile encounter is the flesh so utterly absorbed — and two souls so completely inter-animated — as in the ecstatic feeling that occurs in the mutuality of carnal relations. Here the intimacy of touch viscerally reveals the transcendent possibilities of embodiment — the potential for being myself and being other than or greater than myself. Once more, I recall the words of the poet.

Our bodies why do we forbear? ...
We owe them thanks, because they thus
*   Did us, to us, at first convey,*
Yielded their senses' force to us,
*   Nor are dross to us, but allay.*
On man, heaven's influence works not
so, But that it first imprints the air;
So soul into the soul may flow,
*   Though it to body first repair. (15)*

The feel of my lover's body, the pressure of flesh against flesh, generates heat, stimulating as well our sense of smell and taste, while the tongue, in licking — like the hand, in touching — body's-forth this same cutaneous experience, making direct appeal to appetence and its ready fulfillment. The eyes are perhaps least engaged in this intimate play of flesh with all awareness gathered around touch, smell and taste, and to some extent hearing — listening to a lover's sounds, breathings, and silences.

What is it about touch, and in particular the feel of another's flesh that we find so welcoming and yet, at times, so fearsome? Of course, there is deeply emotional satisfaction in human touch: the hearty handshake, an extended arm to hold, a shoulder to cry on, an affectionate hug, a gentle caress, a loving embrace, or a warm body to envelop me. But there is another, darker side as well: battering, assault, beating, trauma, and the attendant suffering of physical and emotional pain.

The more I reflect on our current historical circumstance, the clearer it seems that the world today is in desperate need of pleasurable touch. Of course human life is and remains mediated — sensual fulfillment always something outstanding, still to be realized anew, again and again. But, it is this very mediation between self and world, or self and other, that gives rise to appetition in the first place. And as Jonas reminds us; like animal being, human existence is essentially passionate. (16)

Throughout my own youth and early adulthood, I never seriously considered the degree to which touch was such an elemental need. But once discovered, never would that recognition be forgotten. And as I later came to see, the primacy of our haptic sense — of touching and being touched — provides the somatic basis for a more organic mode of recollection. In short, there seems to be some primal, if not instinctual, memory-trace associated with tactile sensation itself — a muted, natural recollection buried deep within the folds of my flesh. In their own work, *Sex At Dawn*, Christopher Ryan and Cacilda Jetha are clear about this hard-wired need — not simply for physical connection, but for intimacy as well.

Homo sapiens evolved to be shamelessly, undeniably, inescapably sexual... But these preconscious impulses remain our biological baseline, our reference point, the zero in our own personal number system. (17)

On the other hand, physical isolation, if even for only brief periods, can prove psychologically unsettling — a result of internality, being cut off from normal human interaction — the inability to reach out and touch one another in friendship, intimacy, or even in conflict. Our body of flesh is not so much an accoutrement, additive to our human nature; it is part and parcel of who we are, as well as how we see and position ourselves vis-a-vis one another. Yet, in an increasingly digitized, virtual life-world, further accentuated by the likes of a novel virus, many of us have literally been left desperate for even the most casual experience of human touch. And there is a kind of melancholy tied directly to this inability to reach out and touch one another, to bind ourselves through being together in the flesh.

Today, separated from countless strangers by only thin walls, tiny earbuds and hectic schedules, we assume a desolate sense of isolation must have weighed heavily on our ancestors, wandering over a windswept prehistoric landscape. But in fact, this seemingly common-sense assumption couldn't be more mistaken... The social lives of foragers are characterized by a depth and intensity of interaction few of us could imagine (or tolerate). From the first morning of birth to the final mourning of death, a forager's life is one of intense, constant interaction, interrelation, interdependence. (18)

'Touched by' and 'Cared for'

It would seem in conclusion that we are by nature intertwined, inter-involved and, to that extent, responsible for one another; indeed, this all-too-human burden is reflected in the very structure of our being. We are, as the philosopher says, fundamentally being-there alongside and with other people, even when we are ostensibly alone. This existential structure of being-with implicates us in a profound circle of reciprocity whereby care for the Other — including the sharing of vital resources — seems only natural. (19)   It is simply the human thing to do, rooted in the genetic makeup of the species and our Pleistocene heritage. Martin Heidegger designates this as the essential Care-structure (Sorge) of human existence. It is also significant to note that etymologically 'Care' derives from Old English (*caru*) as well as Old Saxon and Gothic (*kara*) — referring to one's 'concern' or 'anxious apprehension' attendant upon recognition of one's finite nature. In any event, Heidegger reminds us of its import with a fable recorded by Franz Bücheler — a myth concerning the nature of Care.

> *Once when 'Care' was crossing a river, she saw some clay; she thoughtfully took a piece and began to shape it. While she was thinking about what she had made, Jupiter came by. 'Care' asked him to give it spirit, and this he gladly granted. But when she*

wanted her name to be bestowed upon it, Jupiter forbade this and demanded that it be given his name instead. While 'Care' and Jupiter were arguing, Earth arose, and desired that her name be conferred upon the creature, since she had offered it part of her body. They asked Saturn to be the judge. And Saturn gave them the following decision, which seemed to be just:"Since you, Jupiter, have given its spirit, you should receive that spirit at death; and since you, Earth, have given its body, you shall receive its body. But since 'Care' first shaped this creature, she shall possess it as long as it lives. And because there is a dispute among you as to its name, let it be called 'homo,' for it is made out of humus (earth)." (20)

Here we come full circle, acknowledging the tentative and precarious nature of life in the body, accepting the reality of death cradled within our own flesh; at the same time we recognize the world-openness which this concrete body of flesh affords us, including our capacity to touch and be touched by the Other. Herein lies the foundation of our quest for genuine human contact — not only for physical touch and the intimacy afforded by the flesh, but for caring and being cared-for by one another. As Jonas concludes:

> *That life is mortal is indeed its fundamental contradiction, but this also belongs inseparably to its essence. Life cannot at any time be imagined apart from its mortality... [we are] free, but dependent; isolated but in necessary contact; seeking contact, but destructible because of it: conversely, no less threatened by want of contact: endangered thus on both sides, by both the tremendous power and brittleness of the world, and standing on the narrow ridge between. (21)*

Positioned on a kind of precipice — open to the Other, but distracted by my own frailty — I venture out hand-in-hand, bodying-forth my fears as well as my desires, displaying concern as well as my profoundly human capacity to care-for and be cared-for by another.

In the folds of our flesh — wherein the most visceral and engaging state of human existence lies; the very concreteness of life in the body is reflected by our various moods as well as our approach to the Other — anxiety, worry, apprehension, concern and care. Recognition of our own finitude, of our own potentiality for not-being, is what provides the impetus, the desire, to seek out and embrace the Other — to commune, conjoin, and enjoy the camaraderie as well as the intimacy of being together in the flesh. We long for the Other, for connection, for mutual support — to touch and be touched — physically as well as emotionally and psychologically. These are the hallmarks of human life in the body in the world.

Censorship, Historicity, and Self-Understanding

> First they came for the socialists,
> and I did not speak out
> — Because I was not a socialist.
> Then they came for the trade unionists,
> and I did not speak out
> — Because I was not a trade unionist.
> Then they came for the Jews,
> and I did not speak out
> — Because I was not a Jew.
> Then they came for me
> — And there was no one left to speak for me.
>
> Martin Niemoller

I

In the beginning was the 'Woke' Left. Then came 'Cancel Culture.' But before all of this there was simply Political Correctness. And by now we've been advised that certain works in the Dr. Seuss oeuvre are no longer acceptable due to these newly emergent sensibilities. This is not terribly surprising given increasingly repressive views on what's right, good, or appropriate according to newly 'awakened' colleagues. But such assaults on free speech only serve to drive us further down the rabbit hole of censorship, including formal and informal erasure or silencing of significant parts of our cultural history — whether that be institutions, statues, books, opinions, or other people. Yet, what exactly is at stake in this recent phenomenon identified as Woke or Cancel Culture? And what or who is next on the list to be censured?

While this phrase, cancel culture, rolls off the tongue rather effortlessly, what is the actual objective of such a posture? Well, okay; so now we are told that Dr. Seuss' *Mulberry Street* and *If I Ran the Zoo*, among others, will go the way of Mark Twain's *Tom Sawyer* and *Huckleberry Finn*. But is book-banning really the right path down which to travel? Are we now living within the political landscape of an Orwellian novel? Oh, I forgot, even his novel 1984 has been banned repeatedly within the USA. Is this the best way for us to mark the present moment, interpret our past, or plot our future trajectory? And while some correctly recognize that the principle established here opens a pandora's box to further abuses, we clearly see that this box has already been cracked wide open. (22)

Now, all of this began rather innocently enough with one generation's legitimate concern over issues of social and racial justice. However, and as conservatives have been quick to point out, this posture became not simply a banner or a movement, but a cudgel used by progressives, and especially by liberal elites hell-bent on boycotting or silencing anything within our cultural memory they deemed to be objectionable. It is also clear that conservatives latched onto the phrase 'Cancel Culture' as a pejorative label for whatever they saw as progressive views dedicated to silencing specific elements in the cultural memory of America's storied past. Attempting to remain relevant, these conservatives are now pulling out all the stops against the Woke agenda including direct efforts to save or restore elements of our cultural history which the Left has labelled objectionable. So, in the interest of fairness, it is precisely here that we must drill down further and call to task this awakening and any subsequent cancelling.

To better understand and perhaps more appropriately locate this idea of Cancel Culture, we need to be cognizant of changes that have penetrated and helped redirect our cultural dialogue over the past several generations. On the heels of both the feminist and racial-justice movements, we have seen as well the rise of sexual identity politics, not simply gay rights, but an entire alphabet soup comprising the depth and breadth of the LGBTQIA+ community. In short, we have come to see that standard historical and even biological frameworks fall rather short as a means of understanding developing cultural identities and the greater diversity surrounding us. I am not going to suggest here that such movements don't deserve a voice; in fact, they do. I am merely setting the table for us to consider the challenge of cancelling or otherwise erasing dimensions of our own historical trajectory that we no longer like or find redeemable. But, do we really wish to erase significant parts of our cultural heritage in the interests of maintaining some form of political correctness? I propose instead an inclusive rather than an exclusive cultural agenda. I seek to maintain and expand not only cultural diversity, but the very horizon of our cultural understanding. This seems a far better course than trying to restrict the diversity of opinions. So let us proceed with an attempt to understand not only the awakened among us, but the trajectory of a history that requires a fuller accounting in terms of our capacity for self-reflection and self-understanding.

II

There are some preliminary questions to be asked of our Woke compatriots. Have we really been asleep until this very moment in time? If so, to what do we owe this sudden awakening? And, to what exactly have we become awakened? These are not idle queries, but rather go to the very heart of our principal concern: the question of how we come to understand anything whatsoever? In fact, we have a real obligation to inquire about the nature of this awakening — this new understanding. Only then can we decide if those who claim to be woke are really seeing the world anew, differently, or even correctly; or is this perhaps just a means of driving a more subtle and unspoken agenda. Have we really been sleep-walking in America these many years? Or is there something afoot — something we just really have missed?

For their part, a plurality of the Woke crowd appear increasingly ill-at-ease or just plain uncomfortable accepting specific elements of our common cultural heritage. They seem ready to discard elements within the corpus of our collective American memory once they've judged items antithetical to what they feel is socially acceptable. Instead, the most 'progressive' agenda continues to push for jettisoning portions of that history they judge detrimental to their preferred mores — a veritable clutch to control both thought and speech in this brave new world we've come to inhabit. But what is the net effect of this attack on tradition — on our collective memory and cultural history? And what happens if this attack succeeds in erasing even the most marginal elements of our tradition that have been judged problematic by current standards — elements which make members of the newly awakened community uneasy? This would appear to be quite a slippery slope.

This very question serves to remind us of our own historicity, that is to say, our necessary placement within the specific horizon of a concrete cultural tradition. What this means is that our capacity for understanding is itself finite, wholly dependent upon a set of given or pre-existent conditions. This, of course, is due to the nature of human existence itself. We are, in other words, always already situated within concrete temporal circumstances, and that placement remains an ongoing and pre-reflective influence on our capacity for understanding anything whatsoever, including ourselves and other people. In his work entitled Truth and Method, Hans-Georg Gadamer writes:

> *Our attempts to understand... depend upon the questions which our own cultural environment allows us to raise... Our present perspective always involves a relationship to the past... (23)*

As Gadamer reminds us, there is a specific and well-defined horizon — inclusive of our past as well as our current cultural milieu — against which all understanding naturally occurs. This horizon provides the backdrop — Gadamer calls it 'pre-understanding' — as a foundation for grasping the sense of a text, an artifact, any communication or situation whatsoever.

Unpacking this idea, Gadamer further claims that all acts of understanding are guided in advance by certain presuppositions concerning the subject matter at hand — both its relation to my world and how it addresses me personally. In other words, there is no genuine objectivity or impartiality; all acts of understanding are interpretations, both dependent upon and emerging from a foundation of presuppositions already lodged and at work in our pre-understanding. Even the simple act of choosing a topic for investigation is grounded in a pre-thematic grasp of the matter under consideration — guided by pre-conscious attitudes or ways of looking at the world. Gadamer calls these 'prejudices' (a term used without any pejorative sense whatsoever). In other words, we single-out and choose items to consider based upon preliminary, and for the most part, unconscious intuitions or predispositions.

Furthermore, our capacity for understanding the past or even another culture is pre-consciously affected because we always, already find ourselves situated within a specific cultural milieu, a horizon constituting our concrete present along with its prejudices and historical trajectory. This holds true for the individual, the group, as well as the culture as a whole. And while pre-understanding provides the grounding, genuine understanding always occurs by means of a 'fusion of horizons' — of the past with the present, of the alien with the familiar, of my view with that of the Other. It is in this 'fusion' of horizons that the event of understanding truly rests. We are historical creatures, not because we have a history; but the reverse. We have and share in a history because we are fundamentally historical creatures through and through. All understanding is bathed in the waters of this temporal-historical experience.

As Gadamer concludes, the very possibility of having a horizon is due to those pre-conscious prejudices that already help shape whatever we hear, read or otherwise hope to understand. This is the case whether the event under consideration is a dialogue among friends, a homily heard in church, a passage we read in Dostoyevsky, a news clip from across the world, or an aberrant tweet from the White House. Shakespeare had it right when he wrote: "What is past is prologue"; in short, what is past is foundational for our understanding anything whatsoever. Certain underlying cultural predispositions always, already influence the way in which we read any text, hear any words, or otherwise understand a communication, even a casual comment on one's Twitter feed. In this event, any attempt to cancel or erase part of a cultural tradition — texts, history, artifacts, persons — not only destroys the cultural memory, it concurrently eats away at the ground upon which a common understanding is made possible in the first instance. The result of such 'cancellation' is that our present and oftentimes complex culture is transformed into a one-dimensional screen upon which only the latest revisionary spectacle — validated by diligent thought-police — remains available to engage. The remainder, I'm afraid, is lost in a fiery conflagration of burning books, icons and other assorted images.

Understanding within or among diverse cultures is historical at its core. The language, the very terms in which we think and communicate, have a legacy and tradition that cannot be forgotten or ignored. "The past is never dead," wrote William Faulkner; "It is not even past" (24). But, if we allow that to happen, if we allow the past to be erased, if we bend to censorship or its new incarnation — 'Cancel Culture' — we risk allowing key elements of the past to die in this very act of erasure. In that event, a sense of the unfolding historical narrative that helped define our lives both individually and collectively will be disabled and disrupted, leaving the capacity for understanding short-circuited and in large measure without a sound foothold. In brief, we shall find ourselves rudderless, without a grounding narrative arc. If we insist on erasing elements of our cultural tradition, parts of our past — if we try in other words to break or disrupt the circle of understanding that helps ground us — we only succeed in destroying our ability to understand who we are and whence we came. Our ability to see and interpret current events will be cut off from that which has given rise to our present and whatever it is that we genuinely know. It is more than disingenuous if we "aspire to wash away a complicated past and replace it with one that is beyond rebuke." (24)

III

Are there imperfections embedded within the great variety of our culture's historical works or artifacts, whether statues, the arts, texts, personalities, heroes or otherwise? Certainly there are! Seuss or even Twain for example were writing at a different time, under the influence of different cultural norms and sensitivities. But every text necessarily retains the weight and influence of its own concrete placement within a tradition, its own unique history of understanding between its covers. Yet so-called 'flaws' in a work of art or a text are not reason enough for making "the works of important artists disappear…" (25)

Eliminating or silencing such works is not simply censorship. It represents a refusal or failure to acknowledge and engage the self-understanding of the artist or the culture that gave rise to the work in the first place; it betrays our own inability to grasp its relevance or bring the work meaningfully into our current reality thereby inhibiting the expansion of our own horizon of understanding. In fact, it is best when trying to understand the Other — be it a text, work of art, or another person — that we positively engage in a dialogue that can help inform and enlarge our own horizon of understanding, not only of the past but of our current reality as well. This is what helps move us forward, enhancing one's own self-understanding while also enabling one to grasp the other in a continuously expanding circle. It is like an ongoing game, says Gadamer, in which our 'being-with-others' always, already naturally occurs. As the philosopher continues;

> *In speaking with each other we constantly pass over into the thought world of the othe; we engage him, and he engages us. So we adapt ourselves to each other in a preliminary way until the game of giving and taking — real dialogue — begins. (26)*

Gadamer adds, that such a dialogue will always lead to an enrichment of the self, never to its loss or diminution. And these observations hold true for dealing with the written word as well. As he reminds us:

To understand a text is to come to understand oneself in dialogue. a text yields understanding only when what is said in the text begins to find expression in [one's] own language…" (27)

But if we try to silence the text, if we demand the erasure or cancelling of its statement (work or art, statue, personality), we thereby deny ourselves an opportunity to understand our history and our own selves better, more fully; we lose the capacity to enlarge that horizon of understanding. In short, we lose an opportunity for that unique dialogue wherein something new may arise, or as Gadamer summarizes, where something different "comes to be." (28)

Obviously the challenge of recollecting and embracing tradition and historicity are problematic to say the least; we may erase the memory of the KKK for example, but at our own peril. Indeed the re-emergence of far-right anti-government white nationalist movements — among them the Boogaloo Boys, Proud Boys, Three-Percenters, QAnon — now exercising influence over a substantial block of the American electorate indicates just how forcefully our past might come roaring back to dictate the future trajectory of a culture. And while real history is not always to be endorsed or emulated, it certainly needs to be taken account of, if for no other reason than being able to reckon with that tradition as we adjudicate the norms of current and evolving social praxis. In short, the past is never gone but always with us whether or not it we allow it to enlighten or guide us; it is and will always remain prologue.

The Breaking of America's Social Architecture

I

ONCE UPON A TIME in America, citizens had an abiding faith in the strength of their mutual relations — what I will call the 'social architecture' of community. These relationships provided individuals the ability to engage one another within a relatively stable civic environment. Under those conditions the American Dream was alive and well, and running rather smoothly over some well-worn tracks. Such civic engagement was reflected by widespread participation in all manner of public association, including religious congregations, trade unions, chambers of commerce, humanitarian service clubs like Rotary, Lions, and the Kiwanis, as well a host of other broad-based community organizations.

It's important to note that the word "community" derives from two rather ancient Latin roots — *cum* and *munus*; loosely translated it means "to give or share with one another." Yet, perhaps this definition seems rather quaint in today's increasingly competitive environment, in a world where *communio* or 'sharing' suddenly feels more like 'giving something up' or 'giving it away'. Still, as a youth growing up in the late 1950s and early 1960s, I found the evident security provided by community created a safe haven for the enjoyment of everyday life. Simple faith in my community provided a sense of the world and a worldview that was anchored and unshakable. However, as I grew, such assurances seemed to evaporate like hot steam on a cold mirror. Concurrently, the stabilizing effects of communitas slowly began eroding, revealing that this initial faith was perhaps naive. The loss of faith in community has shown that, while people can behave in surprisingly harmonious ways when joined together communicating or collaborating, it also reveals the potential dissonance or madness of the crowd as well.

In his 1970 article published by The New Yorker magazine, Charles Reich — a principal proponent of the '60s counterculture movement and author of The Greening of America — put into rather stark relief what appeared an emergent challenge to the 'social architecture' on whose ground several generations of Americans were nurtured and raised. As he wrote at the time:

> *There is a revolution underway. It is not like revolutions of the past. It has originated with the individual and with culture, and if it succeeds it will change the political structure only as its final act. It will not require violence to succeed, and it cannot be successfully resisted by violence. It is now spreading with amazing rapidity, and already our laws, institutions, and social structures are changing in consequence. Its ultimate creation could be a higher reason, a more human community, and a new and liberated individual. This is the revolution of the new generation.*

While the influence of Reich's revolutionary call should not be minimized, we must also note that he was heralding a revolution without violence; it was a call for a cultural revolution aimed at addressing the issues of personal freedom, political equality, and the future direction of civic life. So, while the foundations of our social architecture were under question, Reich was calling us not to bear arms against one another but rather to engage in debate and dialogue — a collective reassessment of the country's social architecture. In short, he sought expanded the nature of communication within community.

II

Now let us fast-forward to the present day, to the America of a post-Trump presidency. We all watched in amazement and horror on that infamous day while the political grounding of our social architecture was literally being ripped from its moorings by violence; it was an attempt to overthrow our very system of governance. While Reich's Greening, and its consciousness-raising revolution of the 1970s, was a cultural rebellion aimed principally at the Corporate State, this new insurgency was now attacking us not only in city streets but in election boards, governors' offices, and courthouses — including the Supreme Court.   It was a different creature altogether. This new insurgency was an oddly authoritarian intrusion emerging from within a specific segment of the body politic itself, and giving rise to a host of conspiratorial movements.

The rise of groups like QAnon, Proud Boys, Oath Keepers as well as other militaristic or neofascist ideologies, was more than a cautionary tale. According to the Public Religion Research Institute findings earlier this year, nearly 20% of Americans and 25% of Republicans believe in one or more of the QAnon conspiracies. Furthermore, QAnon congressional candidates were on the ballot in at least 26 states as of April, 2022. But this is only the tip of an iceberg that is expanding as it seeks to undermine our commitment to social amity, democratic process, and finally, rationale thought. But let us focus specifically on this QAnon conspiracy and its impact on the presidential transition of 2021.

As a uniquely American millenarian-type cargo-cult, guided by the same presumptions of white privilege seen in its would-be savior, Donald Trump, QAnon thrust into the open several strange and clearly disruptive elements of an undeniably alternative reality. This cult presages a worldview grounded in a rather haunting and anachronistic religious eschatology. It is not surprising then to find blue and white-collar Christians among some of QAnon's most ardent followers, especially among Christian evangelicals. Indeed, this conspiracy has emerged as a reactionary apocalyptic nationalist movement promoting themes that harken back as far as the New Testament's Book of Revelations.

For QAnon believers, marching elbow-to-elbow down the national mall with their white nationalist brethren, Trump represented the 'once and future king' — their anointed savior — his executive role evidenced by fomenting violence in our Capitol. With sticks and stones, guns, body-armor, battering rams, flag poles and bear spray, Trump's cult-followers sought to destroy those who would dare oppose their insurrectionist intentions. With perhaps a touch of irony, and not unlike Jesus's purported overturning of the moneychangers' tables at the Jerusalem Temple, Trump's near mythical status had served to unleash his own legions on our very temple of democracy, seeking to overturn not only the results of the election, but concurrently destroy the foundations of our fragile social architecture.

The symbolism here is both thick and rich. Galvanized by Trump, and prodded on by sycophants like Jake Angeli, their self-anointed shaman, these insurrectionists hammered away at our Capitol as they continued hammering out elements of their own mythically constituted social reality. With a blend of Norse, Neo-fascist, and more archaic imagery, his followers literally sought to carve out a new social architecture, one delivering a new heaven and a new earth, as they imagined it.

For the most part, these disgruntled insurrectionists communicated in a veiled tongue as well, a language laced with both archaic symbolism and novel metaphor. One favorite symbol was that of the Storm, apparently serving as place-holder for an apocalyptic event that would herald the final day of reckoning. This was to be the day when their savior Trump would make his salvific return, exploding across the national stage while the infidels — those blood-drinking pedophiles of the Deep State — would finally receive their long overdue and divinely mandated retribution. Such sentiments bring us awfully close to an eschatological vision of the End Time, much as we find in the New Testament's Revelation of Saint John, and its symbolic representation of 'The Four Horsemen of the Apocalypse'. As we read in Chapter 6 of that book:

I looked, and there was a white horse! Its rider held a bow, and he was given a crown, and he rode out as a conqueror bent on conquest. (6:2)

Then another horse came out, a fiery red one. Its rider was given power to take peace from the earth and to make men slay each other. To him was given a large sword. (6:4)

I looked, and there before me was a black horse! Its rider was holding a pair of scales in his hand. (6:5)

I looked and there before me was a pale horse! Its rider was Death, and Hades followed close behind him. (6:8)

Surely these lines give us pause when considering events surrounding the attempted insurrection on that day. Again, the use of image and symbol is key to QAnon's message, just as we find in St. John's apocalyptic vision. So perhaps — and by way of paraphrase — it may not be too far-fetched to say the following of the former President's assault on the capital, both in his mind and that of his followers. With a crown on his head and scales in hand, he sought to ride out like a conqueror, destroying peace on earth as men slayed one another, leaving death and destruction.

III

It is no accident that QAnon believers are steeped in religious mythology. And given their predilection for apocalyptic eschatology, the energy of this cult has drawn all manner of millennialists and extremists, including white supremacists, evangelicals, and other factions into its fold. But, if we look to the very founding of our nation, the roots of such cult-like activity may already have been growing from the earliest stirrings of white privilege witnessed in the emergence of the 'American Spirit' centuries earlier. And now this same nationalist spirit has been unleashed through the progeny of immigrants whose forefathers had invaded this land centuries earlier.

As suggested above, this is merely the tip of an iceberg that is much larger, and has been growing for longer than we may care to admit. Its origins can be found among those first explorers who dared set foot in the New World, decimating and enslaving its indigenous inhabitants. In short, the mythologically infused movement of that seditious mob in January 2021 may have already been baked into the cake since before our founding and just waiting to explode. And I'm afraid to say that while we've already seen some real fire and brimstone, this volcano may be just about ready to erupt, spewing heated destruction in all corners of our land. I'm fearful that this uneasy but not unlikely alignment or political convergence of a mythico-religious millenarianist movement with a violent and broadly nationalistic conspiracy is leading us fast and furiously to a potentially apocalyptic conclusion. As the congressional representative Donna DeGette remarked in the Senate hearings over a year ago, we now can see "the first stab in a greater revolution."

Circling back to the earlier discussion concerning the destruction of our social architecture, let's now consider a few lingering but critical questions. Is it already too late to coax these mythologically driven reactionaries to engage in some form of reasoned debate; or, has their blind faith in the myth — still tethered to an aggressive neofascist ideology — eclipsed their capacity for discussion and reasoned engagement? Apparently the insurgents have no desire for dialogue or debate. Rather, and in partnership with their far-right-leaning congressional sponsors, they seek hand to hand combat instead. They want to disrupt and ultimately transform an otherwise reasonable socio-political structure into an autocratic religiously driven ideology.

So what should we now expect? And what avenues remain open for meaningful action that may repair or heal our fast-crumbling social reality? I'm afraid there may not be too many more options available, nor the possibility of achieving very much — unless and until we elect politicians blessed with both reason and a genuine capacity for grounded moral judgement. By this, I do not simply mean electing Democrats, but Republicans and Independents as well, anyone who shares our interest in leading both a political and legal movement to protect this country against the threat of an autocratic theocracy. If not, we may be condemned — much like Sisyphus in the myth — to rolling a boulder up the mountain, only to have it tumble back to the bottom each and every time. So, are we simply going to resign ourselves and sit quietly on our hands? Or are there actions we may take, and are there reasons for us to hope against hope that the effort will be fruitful? Perhaps this remains our best, if not our only option.

Notes

1) Hans Jonas, *The Phenomenon of Life: Toward a Philosophical Biology*, p. 19
2) Maurice Merleau-Ponty, *Phenomenology of Perception*, p. 204
3) Ibid, p. 315
4) Ibid, p. 316
5) Ibid, p. 148
6) Ibid
7) Hans Jonas, *The Phenomenon of Life*, p. 12
8) Richard Kearney, *Touch: Recovering Our Most Vital Sense*, p. 47
9) John Donne, *The Ecstasy*
10) See, for example, the study by Chris Ryan and Cacilda Jetha, *Sex At Dawn*
11) Marshall Sahlins, *The Western Illusion of Human Nature*, pp. 46-48
12) Daniel L. Everett, *Don't Sleep There are Snakes*, p. 137
13) Marshall Sahlins, pp. 46-48
14) Hans Jonas, *The Phenomenon of Life,* p. 141
15) John Donne, *The Ecstasy*
16) Hans Jonas, *The Phenomenon of Life*, pp. 106
17) Christopher Ryan and Cacilda Jetha, *Sex at Dawn*, p. 46
18) Ryan and Jetha, p. 87-88
19) See Morton Fried, *The Evolution of Political Society*
20) Martin Heidegger, *Being and Time*, p. 25
21) Hans Jonas, *Memoirs*, p. 230

22) Ross Douthat, "Do Liberals Care If Books Disappear?" *NYT Opinion* Mar 6, 2021

23) Hans Georg-Gadamer

24) William Faulkner, *Requiem for a Nun*

25) Benjamin Wallace, "Who is In Charge of Cancel Culture," *New Yorker,* Mar 11, 2021

26) Elisha Fieldstadt, NBC News, Mar 9, 2021

27) Hans-Georg Gadamer, *Philosophical Hermeneutics*, 57

28) Ibid

29) Ibid, 58

www.ingramcontent.com/pod-product-compliance
Lightning Source LLC
Chambersburg PA
CBHW060538030426
42337CB00021B/4319